On the Front Line

STRUGGLING FOR CIVIL RIGHTS

Stephanie Fitzgerald

Chicago, Illinois

For information, address the publisher:
Raintree, 100 N. LaSalle, Suite 1200
Chicago, IL 60602
Customer Service: 888-363-4266
Visit our website at www.raintreelibrary.com

Printed and bound in China by South China
Printing Company Ltd
09 08 07 06 05
10 9 8 7 6 5 4 3 2 1

**Library of Congress Cataloging-in-Publication
Data**

Fitzgerald, Stephanie.
  Struggling for civil rights / Stephanie Fitzgerald.
    p. cm. -- (On the front line)
  Includes bibliographical references and index.
  ISBN 1-4109-1467-4 (library binding-hardcover) --
  ISBN 1-4109-1474-7 (pbk.)
1. African Americans--Civil rights--History--20th
century--Juvenile literature. 2. Civil rights movements--
United States--History--20th century--Juvenile literature.
3. United States--Race relations--Juvenile literature.
I. Title. II. Series.
  E185.61.F53 2005
  323.1196'073--dc22

                                    2005000134

Acknowledgments
The publishers would like to thank the following for
permission to reproduce photographs:
AKG pp. **6**, **9**, **15**, **23**, **25**; Corbis pp. **4**, **7**, **8**, **11**, **12**,
13, **14**, **16**, **17**, **20**, **22**, **26**, **31**, **32**, **33**, **34**(l), **34**(r), **35**,
37(r), **38**, **41**; Getty images pp. **10**, **21**, **39**, **40**;
Popperfoto pp. **19**, **30**, **36**; Topfoto pp. **title page**,
14(l), **24**, **27**, **28**, **29**, **37**(l).

Cover photograph shows a man being arrested during a
demonstration by the Poor People's Campaign at the
Supreme Court in May 1968, reproduced with the
permission of Corbis.

Map on p. 18 by Jillian Luff.

Source notes: p. **10** Quote from Martin Luther King
taken from *We Shall Overcome: The History of the
American Civil Rights Movement* by Reggie Finlayson;
p. **18** Quote from James Farmer taken from *The Civil
Rights Movement* (Facts on File 1995) by Charles
Patterson; p. **20** Quote from John Patterson taken from
Eyes on the Prize documentary series; p. **22** Quote from
Martin Luther King taken from *We Shall Overcome: The
History of the American Civil Rights Movement* by Reggie
Finlayson and from *Eyes on the Prize* documentary series;
p. **30** Bomb report based on United Press International
(UPI) report, 16 September 1963.

Every effort has been made to contact copyright holders
of any material reproduced in this book. Any omissions
will be rectified in subsequent printings if notice is given
to the publishers.

The paper used to print this book comes from
sustainable resources.

CONTENTS

Any words appearing in the text in bold, **like this,** are explained in the glossary. You can also look out for them in the Word Bank box at the bottom of each page.

A HISTORIC BUS RIDE

In the early 1950s, black people in the southern United States were not allowed to sit with white people on buses. This was called **segregation**. White people sat in the front. Black people sat in the back. Black people could only sit in the middle if no white people wanted those seats. Black people were not even allowed to share the same row as white people.

Rosa makes a stand

On December 1, 1955, a member of the National Association for the Advancement of Colored People (**NAACP**) changed history. Rosa Parks was sitting in the middle of the bus.

Fighting for equality

Black people in the United States wanted equality. They wanted the same rights that white people had. They wanted to be treated just like everyone else. At first, protesters fought to change the laws. Once this had been done they then found that changing people's **attitudes** was even harder.

Rosa Parks walks to jail with her solicitor, Charles Langford (far right), after her arrest for not giving up her seat on a bus to a white man.

Word Bank degrade   treat people as if they are worthless
discrimination   treating people unfairly because of their race, ideas, or beliefs

At first, she did not notice that white people had got on the bus and were left standing. Then the driver told everyone in Rosa's row to get up so a white man could sit down. Three others gave up their seats, but Rosa said no. The bus driver threatened to call the police, but Rosa refused to budge. She was taken off to jail.

Seeds of change

The **degrading** way black people were treated on buses was just one example of the terrible treatment they received all over the southern United States. Treating black people like **second-class citizens** was not even against the law. The civil rights movement fought to change this type of legal **discrimination**.

Find out later

Why were these people protesting?

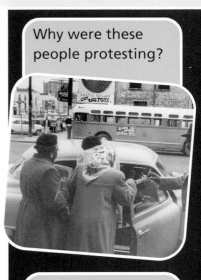

Where and when did Martin Luther King Jr. make his famous "I Have a Dream" speech?

Who came up with the phrase "Black Power"?

second-class citizen someone who does not have the same rights as other people
segregation keeping black people and white people separate

5

SLAVERY AND FREEDOM

Hundreds of years ago, black people were brought to the United States as slaves. They were either kidnapped from their homes in Africa or sold by their enemies. Then they were shipped off to the southern states United States. There they were bought and sold like pieces of property. Slaves had no rights at all. They were forced to work hard for no pay and were often whipped. Slaves could be killed by their owners at any time. The constant threat of violence stopped many slaves from fighting back.

Slavery around the world

Slavery has always existed all over the world. Often, after a battle, the winning side would take their enemies as slaves. But slavery in the United States was different. The people brought from Africa had not been beaten in a war.

Fight for freedom

Not all people agreed with slavery, especially in the North. People who tried to end slavery were called **abolitionists.** One of the first groups of abolitionists in the United States was the Society of Friends, which was formed in the 1750s.

Slaves were often cruelly punished by their masters. This photo, taken in 1863, shows a slave being whipped for trying to escape.

Word Bank   abolitionist   person who fought to get slavery banned
emancipation   being set free

The Civil War

In 1860, the southern states broke away from the rest of the United States, mainly because of disagreements the South had with the U.S. government and the North. The southern army attacked Fort Sumter in North Carolina to start the Civil War (1861–1865). By fighting back, the northern army was trying to keep the country together. In 1862, U.S. President Abraham Lincoln issued the Emancipation **Proclamation.** The Proclamation stated that, as of January 1, 1863, all slaves in the **rebel** southern states would be free. This did not end slavery, but it showed that ending slavery would be an aim of the war.

The Liberator

William Lloyd Garrison was a white abolitionist who started an antislavery newspaper called *The Liberator* in the 1830s. For almost 35 years, until the end of the Civil War, Garrison **lobbied** for the end of slavery and the freeing of all slaves.

Black soldiers fought for the North against the South, which wanted to keep slavery. The abolition of slavery became one of the main issues of the Civil War.

A lifetime of pain

As the Civil War ended in 1865, an **amendment** to the United States **Constitution** was passed making slavery illegal. Other amendments gave African Americans additional rights and freedoms. But black people were still treated unfairly. They were often abused or even killed, just because of the color of their skin. The new laws could not force people to treat each other with respect.

Separate but equal

Once slavery had been outlawed, some white people looked for other ways to control black people. The **Supreme Court** made a ruling in 1896 that gave these people just the chance they needed.

Legal rights emerge

Three amendments to the Constitution gave black people new rights:

January 1865—The 13th amendment made slavery illegal.

July 1868—The 14th amendment made former slaves citizens and guaranteed everyone equal protection under the law.

February 1870—The 15th amendment gave African-American men the right to vote.

In Birmingham, Alabama, in 1940, black people had to sit in a separate balcony at the local cinema.

Word Bank

amendment   change or addition to something
Baptist   religious community that believes in individual freedom

The new ruling said that as long as black people were given facilities that were "separate but equal," they could be kept apart from white people. This meant that black people could not use the same public toilets, water fountains, or schools as white people. All over the country, there were signs for "whites only." Soon, new laws were passed that stated that black people had to use separate facilities from white people. These became known as the **Jim Crow Laws.**

The struggle begins

There had always been strong, brave African Americans in the United States who fought to end injustices, like the **Jim Crow Laws.** But the modern **civil rights** movement really got going in the 1950s. A new generation was coming of age and they were not satisfied to leave things the way they were. Every day, throughout the country, ordinary men, women, and children struggled to change the world.

An important leader

Martin Luther King Jr. was one of the most important leaders of the civil rights struggle. King was a **Baptist minister.** He fought to end **injustice** using nonviolent means, such as peaceful marches and demonstrations.

In the 1950s, people from all over the United States began marching together to end **segregation.**

WALK IN DIGNITY

Rosa Parks' refusal to give up her seat on a segregated bus in 1955 led to the first big protest of the **civil rights** movement. After her arrest, many people decided to **boycott** the bus system in Montgomery, Alabama.

Time for improvement

The Montgomery Improvement Association (MIA) was formed to handle the boycott. Martin Luther King Jr. was asked to be president. The MIA had three demands. They wanted polite treatment on buses. They were willing to sit in the back of the bus, as long as they did not have to give up their seats to whites, and they wanted black drivers for routes in black neighborhoods. Their demands were not met, so the MIA extended the length of the boycott.

An empty bus drives by in Montgomery, Alabama, as people get into a car to ride to work together during the boycott in 1955. ➡

Word Bank boycott refuse to use something
dignity self-respect and pride

Boycott!

Instead of taking buses, 42,000 black residents of Montgomery gave each other lifts, took taxis and walked. To help out, black taxi drivers reduced their fares. Passengers paid the same amount they would have paid for the bus. Some employers who supported the boycott even gave their employees rides to work.

However, the Montgomery authorities were determined to end the boycott. Police threatened the taxi drivers and people sharing cars. They stopped them for driving too fast or too slow. Some employers threatened to fire workers who joined the boycott. Some leaders of the MIA were even arrested. But still no one used the buses. Finally, in December 1956, **segregation** on public buses was made illegal everywhere. The civil rights movement had won an important victory.

Ain't Gonna Ride

This song was sung by the Montgomery boycotters to keep their spirits up.

"Ain't gonna ride them buses no more, Ain't gonna ride no more.

Why don't all the white folk know that I ain't gonna ride no more."

After segregation was outlawed in 1956, Rosa Parks took another ride on the bus. This time she sat in front.

honorable worthy of respect

Segregation was not limited to buses. Black people also faced unfair treatment in schools. School segregation was widely accepted throughout the United States, but was required by law in some southern states. White children always had better schools and books than black children. Black parents went to court to try to desegregate the schools, but they were not successful.

Fighting through the courts

Thurgood Marshall was a lawyer for the NAACP. In 1954,he decided to combine all of the school desegregation cases into one. The case was called *Brown* v. *the Board of Education of Topeka, Kansas.* Before the trial started, psychologists Kenneth and Mamie Clark studied black schoolchildren.

Fighting injustice

The National Association for the Advancement of Colored People (NAACP) was formed in 1909 to fight for racial equality. Since its beginnings, the NAACP has used the court system to fight injustice and promote civil rights.

In 1954, George Hayes (left), Thurgood Marshall (middle), and James Nabrit (right) argued in court against segregation and won.

Word Bank   activists   people who actively support something
appeal   when a court case is taken to a higher court to be heard again

The "doll study"

The Clarks wanted to find out how segregation made black children feel. The psychologists showed the children black and white dolls and drawings. Then they asked which they liked better. The children often picked the white doll or drawing. The psychologists found that even young children thought that being black meant they were of less value in American society.

Separate is not equal

After several losses and many **appeals,** the *Brown* case went before the United States **Supreme Court.** The results of the doll study helped the judges make their decision. They all agreed that "separate but equal" was **unconstitutional.** They said there was no way that something separate could ever really be equal. Segregated schools were ordered to bring African American and white children together.

Non-violent protests

In 1957, the Southern Christian Leadership Conference (SCLC) was formed to co-ordinate the efforts of civil rights **activists.** The NAACP used the legal system to improve civil rights. The SCLC, led by Martin Luther King Jr., on the other hand, organized nonviolent protests and demonstrations.

Even after the courts ordered desegregation, some white schools refused to admit black children. These children were turned away from a white school every day for two years between 1954 and 1956.

desegregate   stop keeping black people and white people apart
unconstitutional   not in agreement with the United States Constitution

The "Little Rock Nine"

The courts had ordered schools to **integrate**. However, many schools in the South refused. In 1957, nine brave black students decided to attend classes at the all-white Central High School in Little Rock, Arkansas despite white protests. The black students were soon attacked, but the "Little Rock Nine" refused to give in.

Left alone

Daisy Lee Bates was president of the Arkansas state conference of the **NAACP**. She was also the students' **escort**. The night before the students were due to enter the school, she tried to call them at home. For safety reasons, they planned to arrive at the school together. But Elizabeth Eckford did not have a phone. She did not know about the plan.

Three brave attempts

It took three tries to get the "Little Rock Nine" into school. First, the governor of Arkansas ignored the court order and ordered the **National Guard** to block the doors. Then, an angry mob drove the students away. Finally, U.S. President Dwight Eisenhower sent in soldiers to escort the students to class.

Black students at Little Rock Central High School had to be protected by army escorts for the first weeks of school.

Through the course of their struggles, the "Little Rock Nine" grew to be very close friends. Here they are studying together.

Word Bank

bayonet   knife that fits in the muzzle of a gun
escort   someone who accompanies and protects another person

A violent mob

Elizabeth showed up for school by herself. She was quickly surrounded by a violent mob. She was not sure what to do, so she tried to go into the school. When she got near the door, a guard stopped her. The guard did not speak to Elizabeth or even look at her. But he raised his **bayonet** as she tried to walk past. People in the crowd started yelling at her and threatening her. Eventually, two white people who were passing by risked their own safety to protect Elizabeth, and walked her back to her bus stop.

Integration

Eventually the campaign of the "Little Rock Nine" forced the Central High School to integrate. By doing so, they opened the door for school **desegregation** throughout the country.

When Elizabeth Eckford tried to enter the school in Little Rock, the crowd screamed insults at her.

Desegregation time line

1954—*Brown* v. *the Board of Education* ruling calls for desegregation of public schools.

1957—The "Little Rock Nine" are admitted to Central High School in Little Rock, Arkansas.

1963—A small number of black students in Alabama, Mississippi, and Louisiana attend public elementary and secondary schools with white students for the first time.

1968—The **Supreme Court** orders states to stop segregated school systems.

1971—The Supreme Court approves the use of buses to make sure that all-black neighborhoods do not lead to all-black schools and vice versa.

integrate   bring everyone together

Although black people and white people could now use buses and schools together, **discrimination** continued. Even in places where **segregation** was not legal, it was a practice based in **tradition**. For example, as part of a deal with the **NAACP**, a national chain of stores had taken down "for whites only" signs at their lunch counters. However, that did not actually change anything as blacks were still not allowed to eat there.

In 1960, Joseph McNeil was going back to his university in Greensboro, North Carolina, after the winter holiday. He was tired, hungry, and thirsty when he got off the bus, but there was nowhere he could sit down to eat. That made him decide to fight segregation at a lunch counter in the town.

Wake up call

One of the "Greensboro Four," Ezell Blair Jr., spoke to a reporter from *The Greensboro Record* named Marvin Sykes on February 2, 1960. He said:

"It is time for someone to wake up and change the situation ... and we decided to start here."

This woman is stopping black people from entering a whites-only lunch counter in Memphis, Tennessee, in 1961.

Word Bank

picketing   marching and carrying signs to protest something
sit-ins   peaceful protests where people sit down and refuse to leave

The "Greensboro Four"

African-American people in Greensboro still had to buy their food at the snack bar and eat it standing up. They were not served at the counters. On February 1, 1960, McNeil and three school friends, Franklin McLain, Ezell Blair Jr., and David Richmond sat down at the lunch counter. The waitress refused to serve them. Still, McNeil and his friends refused to leave. The owner could not have them arrested, so he closed his store early instead.

Success

The next day, the "Greensboro Four" came back with more protesters. The **sit-ins** and **picketing** lasted five months. Finally, the chain of stores agreed to **desegregate** their lunch counters. The success of this sit-in led to others throughout the nation.

SNCC take action

In April 1960, a group of students founded the Student Nonviolent Coordinating Committee (SNCC, called "snick") to plan sit-ins across the country. "Snick" was made up of young people who did not want to become part of older organizations like the NAACP or SCLC. They wanted something new.

Two of the "Greensboro Four" (left and second left), and two friends, sit in protest at a whites-only lunch counter at a store in Greensboro, North Carolina.

tradition way something has always been done

Freedom rides

The same year that the "Greensboro Four" succeeded at ending **segregation** at lunch counters, an African-American man named Bruce Boynton was refused service in a bus station lunchroom. Boynton then sued the State of Virginia and won his case. The **Supreme Court** ruled that segregation in **interstate** bus and train stations was illegal. Again, despite the ruling, most bus stations in the southern United States continued to provide separate lunchrooms, waiting rooms, and rest rooms for black people and white people.

In February 1961, the Congress of Racial Equality (CORE) decided to test the Supreme Court ruling. They would send "freedom riders" onto buses and into terminals throughout the southern United States. The riders would travel from Washington D.C. to New Orleans, Louisiana.

Making news

James Farmer was the founder of CORE. He remembered:

"We had the specific intention of creating a crisis. We were counting on the **bigots** in the South to do our work for us. . . the government would have to respond if we created a situation that was headline news all over the world."

This map shows the routes taken by the freedom riders in 1961.

May 4, 1961 Freedom Ride

May 17, 1961 Freedom Ride

Word Bank   bigot person who dislikes anyone who has different ideas or beliefs from their own

It was planned that as the people were traveling, black freedom riders would use facilities marked for whites only and white riders would use facilities meant for blacks only. Twelve people volunteered to ride the buses. The youngest was 17 years old; the oldest was 61.

Brave volunteers

The freedom riders knew they might be arrested. Each one was ready to go to jail. They also knew there was a very good chance they could be attacked. However, each rider was committed to nonviolent resistance. No matter what happened, they would not meet violence with violence. They would protest with words and actions, but never with fists. They were scared, but they knew what had to be done.

Black and white freedom riders sit together in the "whites only" section of a bus station waiting room in 1961.

interstate travel from one state to another

Into the danger zone

On May 4, 1961, the volunteers and Congress of Racial Equality (CORE) founder James Farmer boarded their buses. At the beginning of the trip, no one really bothered the students. Trouble started as soon as the buses arrived in Birmingham, Alabama. When the riders on one bus reached the Birmingham terminal, there were no police around. That was unusual, and dangerous. In place of the police was a hostile crowd. Some think that Police Chief Eugene "Bull" Connor kept police away so protesters could beat up the freedom riders.. Some riders were attacked and had to be taken to a hospital.

Never give up

When another bus reached the city of Anniston, Alabama, an angry mob surrounded the bus and then attacked it.

These freedom riders in Alabama in 1961 stand helplessly by as their bus burns.

Word Bank enforce make sure a rule is obeyed
federal marshal police officer who works for the United States government

Someone threw a firebomb through a window. As the riders ran from the burning bus, they were beaten up by the crowd. The police refused to help. CORE leaders decided to cancel the rest of the trip. However, new volunteers were ready to continue the ride. When their bus arrived in Montgomery, Alabama, it was met by another angry crowd. Again, many volunteers were beaten up. However, as some of them were injured or arrested new volunteers took their places.

Freedom riders win

The students' refusal to give up brought much attention to the struggle for **civil rights.** That fall, the **Interstate** Commerce Commission issued new rules that would **enforce integration** on buses. **Segregated** bus stations disappeared throughout the South.

Government support

The work of the freedom riders forced the United States government to take a stand on civil rights. President John F. Kennedy supported the civil rights movement and sent **federal marshals** to Alabama to protect students.

U.S. **National Guard** troops protect the bus as freedom riders make the trip from Montgomery, Alabama, to Jackson, Mississippi.

National Guard U.S. military troops who help during emergencies

Protesters normally depend on the police to protect them. But in the 1950s and 1960s, African-American people in the southern United States often feared the police. Some police officers were **racist.** They turned their backs when black people were beaten up. Often, the police even beat up protesters as well.

Time for action

For years, the leaders of the city of Birmingham, Alabama, had refused to support **desegregation.** Police Chief Connor even closed city playgrounds and parks rather than see black people and white people using them together. The extreme racism of many people in the city made it the perfect target for a desegregation project. So, in the spring of 1963, Martin Luther King Jr. and other **civil rights** leaders went to Birmingham.

" Going to jail

With so many people being arrested and sent to jail, Martin Luther King Jr. said:

"... I don't know what to do. I just know that something has got to change in Birmingham. I don't know if I can raise money to get people out of jail. I do know that I can go to jail with them."

Martin Luther King Jr., his wife (right), and son, Martin Luther III, walk to the plane that will take King to jail in Birmingham. ▼

criticize when someone says your actions or ideas are wrong
racism hating a person because of his or her race or skin color

Protests begin

Civil rights leaders decided to try to desegregate lunch counters and other businesses. The protesters staged marches, **boycotts,** and **sit-ins.** They also tried to get black people to register to vote. Police Chief Connor ordered the arrests of hundreds of people. But every day more protesters took the place of those that had been sent to jail.

Locked up!

On April 12, 1963, Martin Luther King Jr. was arrested because he did not stop the demonstrations. He and other protesters were sent to jail. King was **criticized** for his actions in a local paper. His response, "Letter from a Birmingham Jail" (see panel on right), is now considered one of the greatest documents of the 20th century.

Martin Luther King Jr. in a Birmingham jail in 1964.

The Children's Crusade

By May 1963, the leaders of the Birmingham protests were all in jail. Some of the town's black children and young adults decided to take their place on the streets. On May 2, 1963, 1,000 youngsters did not go to school. They met at the Sixteenth Street **Baptist** Church to prepare for a march.

Dogs and violence

As the children left the church, they were taken to jail. By the end of the day, more than 900 children had been arrested. The next day, more children showed up ready to march. Since the jails were full, police let their dogs attack the children and threatened the children with clubs. Firefighters sprayed the children with hoses.

Police set their dogs on a young adult protester during the riots in Alabama in 1963.

Word Bank   terrorize   frighten or scare someone very badly

Parents watched in horror as their children tried to run away but were beaten by police or attacked by dogs. The following Monday, fights broke out between African Americans and whites. Business owners became afraid their stores would be damaged by the fights.

Fragile success

A plan to **desegregate** was finally agreed upon. Business owners also agreed to employ more black workers. But soon after things seemed to settle down, a bomb exploded outside the hotel room where Martin Luther King Jr. was staying. Some witnesses blamed the **Ku Klux Klan** for the attack. African Americans rioted in response. The police then used force against the rioters.

The three 'Ks

The Ku Klux Klan (KKK) is an organization made up of **white supremacists.** It was formed in 1866, and is still active today. Dressed in white robes and hoods, the KKK **terrorized,** even killed, black people without fear of being caught. One of the symbols they used was a burning cross. This picture, taken in 1940, shows KKK members gathered around the cross at one of their meetings.

white supremacist person who believes white people are better than all other races

25

The president speaks up

On June 11, 1963, in response to the Birmingham riots, U.S. President John F. Kennedy went on television. He hoped that he could calm the tensions that had erupted all over the country. Many black **activists,** including a woman named Myrlie Evers, watched the broadcast with increasing hope. Black people had voted for Kennedy because he had promised to support their struggle for **civil rights.** However, until now he had not lived up to that promise. Perhaps now things would change.

Working for the vote

Medgar Evers, Myrlie's husband, worked for the **NAACP** in Mississippi. His focus was the **registration** of black people to vote. The 15th **amendment** gave black men the right to vote although many states used tricks to keep them from the polls.

Barriers to voting

Any white man aged 18 or older could register to vote. They did not have to take a test or pay a tax. But in the southern United States, the law allowed black people to be given impossible literacy tests or forced to pay high poll taxes before they could register to vote.

President Kennedy addresses the nation by radio and television from the White House on June 11, 1963.

Word Bank convicted found guilty of a crime
registration process of qualifying to vote

It was very important for African Americans to vote. Without the vote, they had no say in local or national politics. Without that power they had little hope of seeing the quality of their lives improve.

Evers murdered

Evers had seen people **tortured** and murdered just for trying to vote, but he was determined to change the way things worked in the southern states and make sure all African Americans could vote. As Evers returned from work just after midnight on June 12, 1963, he was shot to death in his driveway. His wife Myrlie heard the gun shot and ran to the door to find her husband crawling toward her. He died shortly afterward.

Three trials

Byron de la Beckwith, a **white supremacist,** was charged with murdering Medgar Evers. His fingerprints were the only ones found on the murder weapon. But juries made up only from white people found him not guilty twice. He was **convicted** by a jury of African-American and white people after a third trial in 1994. He was sentenced to life in prison and died in 2001.

Medgar Evers received a hero's funeral and is buried at Arlington National Cemetery in Washington D.C.

torture   beat or otherwise physically harm

27

March on Washington

For many in the **civil rights** movement, the murder of Medgar Evers was a call to action. They knew that things needed to change quickly. It was time to stage a march on Washington D.C., the nation's capital.

Civil rights **activist** A. Philip Randolph had originally planned a march on Washington in 1941. But President Franklin D. Roosevelt had met Randolph's demand for more jobs for black workers, so the march had been canceled. Now, more than twenty years later, Randolph was planning another march. It would be held on August 28, 1963. Civil rights leaders planned to give speeches that outlined the aims of the movement and raised support for the government's proposed new Civil Rights Act. This would finally do away with the **Jim Crow Laws** and make it illegal to enforce **segregation** in schools, housing, or employment.

Marchers' demands

The marchers' demands included:

- the passing of the Civil Rights Act bill
- **desegregation** in schools
- desegregation in housing
- job training
- an increase in the minimum wage.

Martin Luther King Jr. reaches out to thousands of people at the Washington March in 1963.

Word Bank   creed   person's beliefs, usually religious
inner city   section of a large city, often where poor people live

A peaceful message

Almost every civil rights group came to Washington }for the march. More than 200,000 people of all races and ages took part. Thousands more watched the march on television.

During the day, speakers talked about important things, such as school **segregation,** jobs for African Americans, and money to rebuild **inner cities.** But one of the most moving moments during the march came when Martin Luther King Jr. delivered his "I Have a Dream" speech at the foot of the Lincoln Memorial in Washington D.C. (see panel on right). This speech and the Washington march's peaceful message became the finest hour of the civil rights movement.

"I have a dream"
Martin Luther King Jr.'s speech touched on the broken promise of equality and justice for all. But, more importantly, it also highlighted King's dream of a more promising future.

"I have a dream that one day this nation will rise up and live out the true meaning of its **creed** ... that all men are created equal."

During the march, thousands of people filled the area between the Lincoln Memorial and the Washington Monument in Washington D.C.

Jim Crow Laws laws supporting the segregation of black people and white people, named after a black character in a minstrel show

Innocent victims

The march on Washington left people calm and united in their struggle for **civil rights.** But those good feelings soon went up in smoke. On Sunday morning, September 15, 1963, a bomb blast shook the streets of Birmingham. The bomb had been placed in the Sixteenth Street **Baptist** Church and had exploded just before morning services.

The bomb went off in an empty basement, blasting a huge hole in the wall. Pieces of brick and glass were sent flying into a nearby classroom, where children were getting ready for church. More than twenty people were injured, and four girls were killed. Denise McNair was just 11 years old. The other victims, Cynthia Wesley, Carole Robertson, and Addie Mae Collins, were all fourteen years old.

A man kneels after the Sixteenth Street Church bombing in Birmingham, Alabama, praying for the children that died. ➡

Anger and riots

The bombing of the church led to riots. Some angry black people attacked white people and destroyed many businesses owned by white people. Others, including Denise McNair's father, begged people to stay calm. By the time the violence was over, two more black children had been killed. A 16-year-old boy had been shot in the back by police and a 13-year-old boy had been killed by two white teenagers.

Justice delayed

The United States government did not want the men thought to be responsible for the bombing to be sent to jail. Federal Bureau of Investigation Director J. Edgar Hoover blocked the prosecution of suspects because it would be too hard to get a conviction. Finally, in 1977, one suspect was tried and **convicted**. In 2001, a second suspect was found guilty and, in 2002, a third. All were sentenced to life in prison. The fourth suspect died before being tried.

Too many bombs

Between 1957 and 1963 there were eighteen unsolved bombings in black neighborhoods in Birmingham, Alabama. This earned the city the nickname "Bombingham." Some people believe that the fact that all these crimes went unsolved shows how little white officials cared about violence against blacks.

During the riots in Birmingham, Alabama, in 1963 the police used armored trucks to try to keep the peace.

Pushing for votes

By the mid-1960s, the **segregation** of African Americans and white people had been ended and black people had more rights than ever before. But still many African Americans were not able to vote. For example, black people made up half of the population of Selma, Alabama, but only one percent of them were **registered** to vote. In 1965, student organizations decided to march from Selma to Montgomery, Alabama's capital. Once they reached the capital, **civil rights** leaders would present a list of complaints to Alabama's leaders and demand **reform.**

Two very different marches

The protesters started marching on Sunday, March 7, 1965, but were stopped at the edge of the city by state police. The officers ran through the crowd, swinging their clubs and shooting tear gas. Many protesters were injured as violence broke out.

When the Selma marchers started out on March 7, 1965, they were faced by a wall of police.

Word Bank   oversee   take charge of something
passive   refusing to use violence to settle arguments

The protesters were determined to carry on. Two days later, they began their march again. This time, when they reached the police, Martin Luther King Jr. asked the protesters to kneel and pray. When they got back up from praying, King led them back to their starting point. Some of the protesters felt let down by King's **passive** reaction. But he asked them to be patient a bit longer.

Success at last

About 3,200 people, black and white, began to march to Montgomery again on March 21, 1965. This time, **federal marshals** were there to protect them. By the time they reached the capital, the group had grown in size and there were 25,000 people. They presented their complaints to the governor.

Thousands of demonstrators joined King (center) on his march to Montgomery.

reform change for the better

March against fear

On June 5, 1966, a black **activist** named James Meredith began a 220-mile (354-kilometer) march from Memphis, Tennessee, to Jackson, Mississippi. He had chosen a very dangerous route for a black man to walk. Black people in Mississippi lived in fear of **racist** attacks. Meredith hoped that his march would free people from that fear. He also wanted to encourage people to **register** to vote.

Meredith is shot

On the second day of his walk, Meredith was shot. He fell next to the road and was rushed to the hospital. Major **civil rights** organizations promised to continue Meredith's march. They started from the point where he was shot. Hundreds of people gathered to carry on the march, and Martin Luther King Jr. urged them not to use violence in their protests.

University riots

The 1966 march was not the first time James Meredith had made the news. In 1961, Meredith (pictured below) was accepted into the all-white University of Mississippi. He was given the protection of **federal marshals** on his first day at the University. On the day he tried to register for classes about 2,000 people rioted. Two people were killed and 160 injured. It took more than 20,000 troops to calm things down. Meredith graduated in 1964.

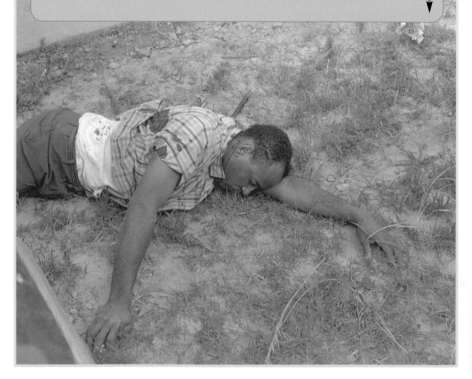

Close to the start of his march, James Meredith was shot. In this picture, he lies wounded on the ground. Meredith survived, and was able to march again.

Word Bank cooperation working together

The use of force

But times had changed. Younger members of the civil rights movement, like Stokely Carmichael, were tired of King's peaceful approach. They were tired of waiting for white people to give them what they deserved. They felt they had to take it by force. For these new protesters, it was time to use violence if necessary.

Meredith returns

As the march peacefully moved through Mississippi, Carmichael preached the need for power. He even made the phrase "black power" his slogan. Meredith felt well enough to join the march again in Jackson. By the end of the 22-day trip, he and other marchers had encouraged almost 4,000 black people to register to vote.

Black power

Many young activists had lost faith in the "old" ways. They thought that **cooperation** with whites would not work. Instead, they believed in making progress through independent black power. They had to take what they wanted, not wait for someone to give it to them.

Stokely Carmichael was a very powerful speaker.

Meredith's march in June 1966 was the last time the major **civil rights** groups were completely **unified** in their struggle for civil rights. After that, many younger members of the movement took a more **militant** position.

Many more riots

The mid-1960s were troubled times. Many riots were started because of violence between police and blacks. The 1964 Harlem riot in New York, for example, began when an off-duty police officer shot and killed a 15-year-old black boy. The 1965 Watts riot in California began after a black motorist was stopped and **subdued** by police. The watching crowd was angered by the police brutality and was soon out of control.

In response to these and other incidents all over the United States, radical new organizations were set up by militant black **activists**. The Black Panther Party for Self-Defense was formed in October 1966. The Black Panthers carried weapons and encouraged members of the Party to defend themselves.

Olympic salute

During the medal ceremony at the 1968 Olympic Games, two African-American sprinters gave the black power salute as the U.S. national anthem played. The athletes were named Tommie Smith (below left) and John Carlos (below right). They also stood with bare feet to represent slavery and **discrimination,** and bowed their heads to show that black people were not free. The International Olympic Committee punished them by taking away their medals.

36

Word Bank   militant   fighting in a very aggressive way
separatist   person who believed in keeping people apart

Another group, the Nation of Islam, did not agree with black people and white people living side-by-side. They encouraged black people to form their own society. They wanted to live separately from whites. This idea was called black separatism.

Tired of violence

By the late 1960s, most Americans were growing tired of the violence. More and more people were deciding not to support the black **separatists.** The focus of the nation began to move from the struggle for civil rights to protesting against the Vietnam War. Martin Luther King Jr., for example, spoke out against the war many times.

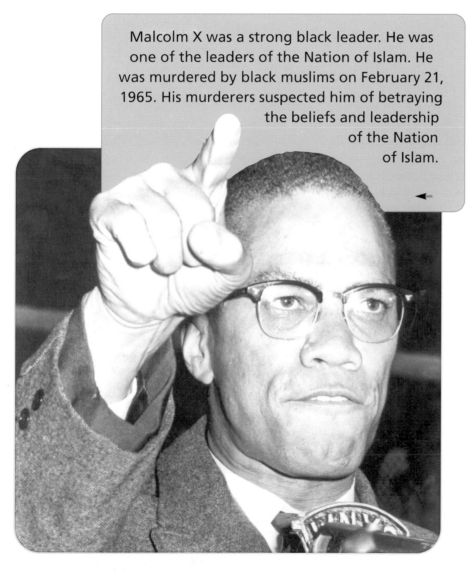

Malcolm X was a strong black leader. He was one of the leaders of the Nation of Islam. He was murdered by black muslims on February 21, 1965. His murderers suspected him of betraying the beliefs and leadership of the Nation of Islam.

The Black Panthers

In the photo above, Black Panthers march in their trademark black berets. The flags carry a picture of their symbol, the black panther. Black Panthers believed they had a right to take what they wanted by force if necessary. Some of their main aims included:

- stopping police brutality

- making good housing available to black people

- teaching people black history.

subdue control by force
unified acting together with a single aim

Focus on poverty

By the late 1960s, even **traditional activists** were changing their focus. Unfair laws had been challenged and changed. But no law could ever force American society to see blacks as completely equal. Instead, people's opinions had to change.

The garbage collectors

Martin Luther King Jr. realized that it was not enough just to change laws, he wanted to change lives. Many black people lived in terrible poverty and this was hurting them just as much as **segregation** once had. Because of this, King decided to campaign for the garbage collectors in Memphis, Tennessee, in 1968. They were paid very little and lived in awful conditions. He wanted better wages and better living conditions for black workers like these. Tragically, King did not live to see these things happen.

Martin Luther King Jr. campaigned to reduce poverty amongst black families like this one.

Shot dead

When King spoke on April 3, 1968, he talked about the threat of violence and his hope for better days. "Like anybody, I would like to live a long life," he said. "But I'm not concerned about that now. I just want to do God's will. And he's allowed me to go up to the mountain. . . . And I've seen the Promised Land. I may not get there with you. But I want you to know tonight. . . . I'm not worried about anything. I'm not fearing any man." The next day, Martin Luther King Jr. was shot dead as he stood outside his hotel room. A man named James Earl Ray confessed to the murder and was sentenced to 99 years in prison.

> Martin Luther King Jr. lies on the balcony of his hotel after being shot. Civil rights leaders, including Dr. Ralph Abernathy and Jesse Jackson, point to where the gunshots came from.

Set up?

When he was arrested, James Earl Ray admitted to killing Martin Luther King Jr. A few days later, though, he claimed he was framed. Some people believe that Ray did not act alone. Even so, the police were sure that Ray fired the shot that killed King.

New attitudes

The 1950s to early 1960s were very important years, because so much had to be done. African Americans in the United States had very few rights. During this time great changes happened. As far as the legal system was concerned, black people became equal citizens. However, a person's **attitudes** toward other races cannot be controlled or forced to change through laws.

Positive change

Over the years, the United States government has tried to make up for the inequality that still remains between black and white people. The government has made many changes.

Thousands of heroes

There are thousands of heroes of the **civil rights** movement. Many ordinary people risked their lives to help others live better ones.

Jobs such as teaching are now much more open to black people, who in turn teach mixed-race classes.

Word Bank   legacy   something important left to a person by or as if by will

Schools and businesses now have to accept a certain number of **minority** students and workers by law. This is called affirmative action.

Civil rights legacy

Although some people feel that affirmative action is not the perfect answer, others say that it is at least an attempt to make things right. A great **legacy** of the civil rights movement is that it changed the way people think about others. People have the ability to learn and grow. As long as we continue to do so, we may still see the day where no one is judged by such a thing as the color of their skin.

Blacks in power

In 1967, Thurgood Marshall became the first black **Supreme Court** Justice. In recent years, the United States has seen the appointment of Colin Powell as the first black Secretary of State and Condoleezza Rice as the first black woman Secretary of State.

Today, children of all races live and learn side-by-side.

minority   small group of people who share something in common, such as race or religion

TIME LINE

1861
January
April

The South secedes from the United States of America. Confederate Army attacks Fort Sumter in North Carolina. The Civil War begins.

1863
January 1

President Abraham Lincoln issues the **Emancipation Proclamation.**

1865
January
May

Thirteenth **amendment** makes slavery illegal.
General Robert E. Lee, the leader of the Confederate Army, surrenders to Union leader General Ulysses S. Grant. The Civil War is over.

1868
July

Fourteenth amendment makes former slaves citizens and guarantees everyone equal protection under the law.

1870
February

Fifteenth amendment gives African-American men the right to vote.

1954
May 17

Brown v. *the Board of Education of Topeka, Kansas* ruling states that **segregation** in public schools is **unconstitutional.**

1955
August

Fourteen-year-old African American Emmett Till is murdered after whistling at a white woman.

December 1

Rosa Parks is arrested for refusing to give up her seat on a bus.

December 5

Montgomery bus **boycott** begins.

1956
December 21

Buses are **desegregated.**

1957
September 25

The "Little Rock Nine" end segregation at Central High School.

1960

December 5   Segregation in **interstate** bus terminals is ruled unconstitutional.

February 1   The "Greensboro Four" begin their **sit-in** at a segregated lunch counter.

1961

May 4   Freedom rides begin.

1963

June 12   Medgar Evers is murdered outside his home.

August 28   March on Washington is held.

September 15   Bombing at the Sixteenth Street **Baptist** Church kills four girls.

1964

July 2   President Johnson signs the **Civil Rights** Act of 1964, making segregation in public facilities and **discrimination** in employment illegal.

1965

February 21   Malcolm X is shot to death in Harlem.

March 7   Selma march begins.

August 10   Congress passes the Voting Rights Act of 1965, which stopped literacy tests as a qualification for voting and appointed federal examiners with the power to register people to vote.

1966

June 5   James Meredith starts his march.

1968

April 4   Martin Luther King Jr. is assassinated.

April 11   President Johnson signs the Civil Rights Act of 1968, prohibiting discrimination in housing.

1988

March 22   Congress passes the Civil Rights Restoration Act, which expanded the laws supporting non-discrimination.

1991

November 22   President George H.W. Bush signs another Civil Rights Act that strengthened civil rights laws banning discrimination in employment, among other things.

FIND OUT MORE

Search tips

There are billions of pages on the Internet so it can be difficult to find exactly what you are looking for. These search skills will help you find useful websites more quickly:

- Use simple keywords instead of whole sentences.

- Use two to six keywords in a search, putting the most important words first.

- Be precise – only use names of people, places or things.

- If you want to find words that go together, put quote marks around them.

Books

Here are just a few of the many books about the struggle for civil rights.

Anderson, Michael. *The Civil Rights Movement*. Chicago: Heinemann Library, 2004.

Downing, David. *Malcolm X*. Chicago: Heinemann Library, 2003.

Finlayson, Reggie. *We Shall Overcome: The History of the American Civil Rights Movement*. Minneapolis: Lerner Publications, 2003.

Fireside, Harvey. *The Mississippi Burning Civil Rights Murder Conspiracy Trial*. Berkeley Heights, NJ: Enslow, 2002.

Fraden, Judith Bloom and Dennis Brindell. *Daisy Bates and the Little Rock Nine*. Boston: Clarion, 2004.

Gogerly, Liz. *The Dream of Martin Luther King*. Austin, Tex.: Raintree Steck-Vaughn, 2004.

McWhorter, Diane. *A Dream of Freedom: The Civil Rights Movement from 1954–1968*. New York: Scholastic, 2004.

Schraff, Anne. *Rosa Parks: Tired of Giving In*. Berkeley Heights, NJ: Enslow, 2005.

St. Lawrence, Genevieve. *Medgar Evers*. Chicago: Raintree, 2004.

Organizations

The April 4th Foundation
tel.: (901) 276-6761
email: info@aprilfourthfoundation.org

The April 4th Foundation organizes and supports historical and educational programs that coincide with the anniversary of Dr. Martin Luther King's assassination. The organization also promotes community and national development programs supporting civil rights. Contact them for a schedule of events.

NAACP
4805 Mt. Hope Drive
Baltimore, MD 21215
tel.: (877) 622-2798

Founded in 1910, the National Association for the Advancement of Colored People (NAACP) was the first civil rights movement in the United States. Contact them to get involved or for more information.

Museums

The National Civil Rights Museum
450 Mulberry Street
Memphis, TN 38103
tel.: (901) 521-9699

The Rosa Parks Library and Museum
Troy State University Montgomery
251 Montgomery Street
Montgomery, AL 36104
tel. (334) 241-8661

Where to search

Search engine

A search engine looks through the entire web and lists all sites that match the words in the search box. It can give thousands of links, but the best matches are at the top of the list, on the first page. Try **google.com**

Search directory

A search directory is like a library of websites that have been sorted by a person instead of a computer. You can search by keyword or subject and browse through the different sites like you look through books on a library shelf. A good example is **yahooligans.com**

GLOSSARY

abolitionist person who fought to get slavery banned

activist person who actively supports something

amendment change or addition to something

appeal when a court case is taken to a higher court to be heard again

attitude idea or opinion

Baptist religious community that believes in individual freedom

bayonet knife that fits in the muzzle of a gun

bigot person who dislikes anyone who has different ideas or beliefs than their own

block street

boycott refuse to use something

civil rights freedoms within a country that all people should be granted

Constitution set of laws and beliefs used to guide and run the U.S. government

convicted found guilty of a crime

cooperation working together

creed person's beliefs, usually religious

criticize when someone says your actions or ideas are wrong

degrade treat people as if they are worthless

desegregation stop keeping black people and white people apart

dignity self-respect and pride

discrimination treating people unfairly because of their race, ideas, or beliefs

emancipation being set free

enforce make sure a rule is obeyed

escort someone who accompanies and protects another person

federal marshal police officer who works for the United States government

honorable worthy of respect

humiliated feeling that you are not as good as everyone else; made to feel ashamed

injustice when people are treated unfairly

inner city section of a large city, often where poor people live

inspiration something that sets a good example for others to follow

integrate bring everyone together

interstate travel from one state to another

Jim Crow Laws laws supporting the segregation of black people and white people, named after a black character in a minstrel show

Ku Klux Klan (KKK) white supremacist group that terrorized black people in the southern United States

legacy something important left to a person by or as if by will

lobby try to get people to agree with you

militant fighting in a very aggressive way

minister preacher in a church

minority small group of people who share something in common, such as race or religion

NAACP (National Association for the Advancement of Colored People) one of the earliest civil rights organizations that used the U.S. legal system to bring about change

National Guard U.S. military troops who help during emergencies

oversee take charge of something

passive refusing to use violence to settle arguments

picketing marching and carrying signs to protest something

proclamation official announcement

psychologist person who studies human behavior

racism hating a person because of his or her race or skin color. A person who hates other people because of their race or skin color is called a racist.

rebel fighting against the government or authority

reform change for the better

registration process of qualifying to vote

second-class citizen someone who does not have the same rights as other people

segregation keeping black people and white people separate

separatist person who believed in keeping people apart

sit-in peaceful protest where people sit down and refuse to leave

subdue control by force

Supreme Court top legal institution in the United States

terrorize frighten or scare someone very badly

torture beaten or otherwise physically harm

tradition way something has always been done

unconstitutional not in agreement with the United States Constitution

unified acting together with a single aim

white supremacist person who believes white people are better than all other races